DEDICATIONS FROM THE HEART

Edited by

Heather Killingray

First published in Great Britain in 1999 by
POETRY NOW
1-2 Wainman Road, Woodston,
Peterborough, PE2 7BU
Telephone (01733) 230746
Fax (01733) 230751

HB ISBN 0 75430 600 3
SB ISBN 0 75430 601 1

FOREWORD

Although we are a nation of poetry writers we are accused of not reading poetry and not buying poetry books: after many years of listening to the incessant gripes of poetry publishers, I can only assume that the books they publish, in general, are books that most people do not want to read.

Poetry should not be obscure, introverted, and as cryptic as a crossword puzzle: it is the poet's duty to reach out and embrace the world.

The world owes the poet nothing and we should not be expected to dig and delve into a rambling discourse searching for some inner meaning.

The reason we write poetry (and almost all of us do) is because we want to communicate: an ideal; an idea; or a specific feeling.

Poetry is as essential in communication, as a letter; a radio; a telephone, and the main criteria for selecting the poems in this anthology is very simple: they communicate.

CONTENTS

A DAUGHTER'S LOVE

I saw you hurting
I felt your pain
I watched you cry those tears again

All I could do is offer
My two arms to embrace you
And perhaps it might have helped you through

I see you hurting
I feel your pain
I watch you cry those tears again

All I can do is offer
My two arms to embrace you
And perhaps it might help see you through

I'll see you hurting
I'll feel your pain
I'll watch you cry those tears again

And all I will do is offer
My two arms to embrace you
And perhaps it might help to see you through.

All my love always mum.

Ann Burgess

DEDICATED TO BERNIE AND BRIAN HAYES

Mum and Dad you're so very far away
To you, there is so much for me to say
I know we've had our ups and downs in the past
But the bad memories are not the ones that last
It's the fun and laughter that we all did share
The feelings of love and showing we care
These are the things we hold onto that mean so much
And I'm glad to say that we have never lost touch
I'd live to thank you for the upbringing that I had
For you both being an understanding Mum and Dad
Teaching me the difference between right and wrong
Helped me choose the path of life, however long
Giving me comfort when in need, and a smile to cheer
Made me feel so important and to you so dear
As years passed by, separate ways we had to go
At times it made me feel so desperately low
It's the future now that I look forward to the most
When it's me that can take over the role of the host
After ten years apart, together we all will be
When you make that journey back home across the blue sea
We can all pick up the pieces and join again as one
And remember all the happy things that were said and done
It will be a time for us to get close again too
And for me to say those special words of 'I love you!'

Penny Brown

To Walk With You

I would like to walk with you
Along the ridged sand of a northern beach
With the hiss and roar of the ebb-tide
And the stinging sea spray
Swirling about our ears.

I would like to walk with you
Across a high and windy moor
With tough tentacles of heather tugging at our feet
And ahead of us a grass-grown road
Towards our destination.

I would like to walk with you
In the crowded streets of a town
Surrounded by a heaving sea of strangers
Pushed and pulled by the press of bodies
And your hand fast in mine.

I would like to walk with you
Through the flowering woods in springtime
Along the June hedgerows at evening
Across the singing summer fields
And then to bring you home.

Helen Parsons

DEDICATED TO THE MAN I WILL ALWAYS LOVE

Tender glances fill the air
As my life love, Oh! so fair
Watches me with eyes of blue
Laughing merrily in the morning dew
No one else can take your place
With your wonderful thoughtfulness and grace
When you walked with me in the spring
When the year's happiness can begin
Whitty words that only you beguilely
Utter to make me overflow with delight and butter
Often would not melt in your mouth
But still my loving heart forever forgave you
We both would enjoy the banter
And would know we could overcome the trying matter
Oh! for the days of yesteryear
When my heart was in full splendid gear
Waking with the one I dearly loved beside me
A morning kiss would leave me as a spirit free.

Alma Montgomery Frank

To Charles

You're a friend to everyone
Whether large or small,
Age is immaterial,
You're special to us all.

The tinies know you love them
As they sit upon your knee,
Assured you will be gentle
They're as happy as can be.

With no inhibitions
They put their arms round you,
And whisper softly in your ear,
Planting a kiss or two.

As for us older ones,
We like your courtesy
And kind consideration
Whoever we might be.

You're always on the lookout
To make people smile
With a charming, merry quip,
As you chat awhile.

To some you're very faithful
When we're feeling ill,
A regular daily phone call
Helps to sweeten the pill.

So, Charles, go on being
A real gentleman,
Bringing joy and love to all
In every way you can.

Rita Hardiman

WRONG PLACE WRONG TIME
(Dedicated to Steve
Right person, wrong time)

A feeling of trust
from when first we met
Not sure why at least not yet
Wanting to say I'd like to get to
                    know you better
not knowing if I'd just get a red letter.
To listen to my instincts I'd say you
                         feel the same
How I long to hear you whisper my name
Yet somehow I feel it's just your job
Maybe you care about what you do
Maybe you will call or drop by
I trust and want to talk to you so much
I just can't figure out why.

Yvette Herbert

To You

This is dedicated
to the one I love

This is translated to the
one I see

This is annotated to the one I sense
but never open to.
Who never sees the real me or
notices my shy blushes
or twisting
body language.

This is camouflaged to the one
I could love
if he let me
but the one I fear
because he won't.

Amber Agha

MEN AT CHRISTMAS

We don't want frilly knickers
or chocs to make us fat
We don't want a new Hoover
and we don't want a cat
We don't want a workmate
or an electric drill
We don't want a sander
or the credit card bill
We don't want a dress
that is three sizes too small
Use your imagination
you've no idea at all
We don't want cheap rubbish
oh and listen dearest honey
Don't get your mum to buy it
just give us some flippin' money.

Joy Benford

OUR MOTHER DEAR

Mother Dear,

We are writing now to tell you, as another year has turned,
and as Xmas now approaches, that it's a day for which we've
long yearned.
When we snuggle around our Xmas tree, which sparkling
baubles will adorn, and with rooms so filled with your presence
there, it's happiness reborn.
With your warmth to give us comfort, which we know is always dear,
there's your open arms and open heart, and your ever-listening ear.
What would we do without you, your family now widespread,
Without our little kiss on cheek, and your shoulder to rest our head.

So now we want to tell you, how lonely it would be, if Mother dear,
you were not there, to spread love to your family.

Alan Smith

TO MURIEL AND MARION OUR COUSINS IN CANADA

We cannot span the ocean wide
to shake you by the hand,
but telephone's at the bedside;
it is a magic wand

when activated waves your voice,
so near and yet so far,
with thanks to Graham Bell; our choice
is asking how you are.

You've had the summer warm, you say;
wish we could say the same.
Here summer came in early May;
the weather is to blame.

It's now gone fifty years, and more,
while still in Air Force blue,
I trained in 'Ansons' during war,
at school called Mountain View.

I wintered well in Canada
with sleigh bells and the snow;
then out-of-bounds were Regina
and Vancouver also.

Sorry to hear about your 'ops'
in hospital, you tell;
let's hope the cooler inside air
had helped to get you well.

From your cousins Hilda and me
at this time of the year
best wishes and we hope you'll be
hale and no worse of wear.

Struan Yule

MY SISTER

Little hands bedecked with jewels
so soft and warm to touch.
A gentle smile and sparkling eyes
with many a tale to hide.
With eyes so keen the lighter side seen
and laughs from deep within.
Hidden deep the pain of heart and limb
by a body frail, shackled, yet with a spirit free.
A heart so full and bursting with love
Eager and ready to lend a hand.
Ears to listen for a whispered plea
to hear the words uttered, yet never spoken.
All of these, and still some more
a friend, so true and loyal.
Through skies of grey and rays of sun
an icon of delight - my sister so dear!

John Wynn

I SHOULD BE

I should be dedicated to
Loving someone just like you
But I was a fool and let them go
Though I have always loved you and now I know.

I should be dedicated to
Getting to know again someone like you
Who really has shown me the way ahead
A different story of life ahead.

I should be dedicated to
Buying a gift to surprise you
To try and win you over to my side
And convince you I am not telling lies.

Keith L Powell

DEDICATED TO MY AFRICAN FRIEND

The time has come, once again,
For us to get in touch
The Christmastime we spent together
I think about so much.

Time then had come for us to say goodbye
Could not hold back the tears
We threw streamers in the air
And while they swirled and curled around us
Making patterns everywhere
You drove away in the car
Leaving me to care.

We knew not when we'd meet again
The years fly by so fast
But wipe away the tears, bring back a smile
Distance can't divide us
Friendship means a lasting, precious thing
I will write to you tomorrow
Dispel sorrow.
Who knows what life will bring?

So once again I take my pen
And wish you all the best
This Christmastime
Remembering fifty years since our
Friendship's test.

P M Burton

IS IT THIS THING CALLED LOVE?
(Dedicated to Martyn Barrington Drake)

I crave his companionship,
But I do not desire him.
Still, from the time we first met
He is such a Gentleman,
I happen to like dat.
And we have lots in common.
So should I call it love,
Or just good friendship?

Of course it's the latter.
But I dunno the former.
Yet he of me reminds,
Lyrics by: Ira Gershwin,
Yip Harburg, Irving Berlin,
And Oscar Hammerstein's
Writings about love!

He has me in a spin.
I do not desire him,
Just crave his companionship.

Emma Dorothy Shane

THOUGHTS UNSAID
(Dedicated to my sister Nell)

The thoughts we had,
The things we never said.
How oft we keep deep thoughts within our head.
If we had said
The things we really thought
Our lives would be so different
and, maybe, not so fraught
With tears and rage, sorrow and
recriminations.

We could have turned another page
And said, 'I love you . . .'
And really meant it;
Instead of holding back
And letting pride prevent it.

Now years have passed
And eyes grow dim.
Our bodies are decaying
But thoughts are still within.
So, let us say while there is time
The things we left unsaid;
And bring a glow of happiness
And peace of mind, instead.

Betty Wildsmith

MUM AND DAD

Mum, Dad, this ode's for you
It's dedicated as I write
To express the way I feel
About you both, day and night

You both mean such a lot
I love you both so dear
You're always there for me
Through happiness or tears

I remember many ways
You made me feel good
And hold much respect for you
To my heart, you're food

Your tireless thoughts and little ways
Of giving me some hope
To hold onto when in strife
Helped me to cut my rope

So I wanted you to know
How much I love you two
And I will always hold you near
I'm lucky having both of you

So, many thanks and much love
I send in these few deep lines
Along with a lot of pride
In knowing you're both mine.

Fiona McCulloch

CHRISTMAS PAST

This Christmas may be the last
we have together as a
family. Your place is so
strong. It reflects the glow of
candlelight shining on the
smooth, glass spheres of blood-red
tree baubles. Fragile trifles
can never be compared to
the wealth in my heart, as I
look back over the years
we have had together from
'nappies' till now. One long round
of problems, gems of goodness
and sheer humanity.
As that special mother long
ago, once stored memories
in an aching heart, against
a painful, unknown future,
your life, dear Son, is saved
in red blood; encased in the
tenderness of our Christmas.

Elizabeth Goffin

MY LOVE
(Dedicated to my wife Sylvia)

The sky is clear, no cloud in sight,
My love for you is forever bright,
The sound of the gentle breeze we hear,
Our hearts entwined as we grow ever near.
Spring with bright and cloudless days
For us to share, in all kinds of ways;
Summer sun and clear blue skies
For us together our love will never die;
Autumn brings the winds and falling leaves.
We'll just cuddle up against the chilling breeze;
Winter's on us now, so cold and drear,
We'll sit together with thoughts and memories
we hold so very dear.

D C J Jones

NOSTALGIA

When I hear your voice, so gentle,
Singing of those distant isles,
My thoughts at once wax sentimental
And bridge the gap of all the miles
Between us, and the spots where often
We used to wander hand in hand.
As the light of day would soften
Into twilight, and the sand
Silvery in the glow of moonlight,
A kaleidoscope of gleaming gems,
Where the moonbeams of the short night
Wove their effulgent diadems.
Then, my heart within me burning,
Yearning to get back once more,
Would that we were now returning,
Returning to that magic shore.

A Maciver

ONE LOVE FOREVER
(Dedicated to Diane)

For many years you graced my life
With beauty, charm and song.
Our love was sweet and strong;
Oh how for you I long,
My lover and my wife.

You moved up to a higher plane
Yet always you are near;
I often shed a tear,
Without you, life's austere.
Is there no end to pain?

I know one day we'll meet once more,
For love still reigns supreme.
This is no futile dream,
Forever we're a team.
We'll meet at Heaven's door.

Francis Marshall

FIRST LOVE
(For Kevin Whitehead)

Alderley Edge, with the sun shining down,
You and I in the park in the centre of town.
Your face and your smile, and those feelings I miss,
Our innocent love, that knew only a kiss.
Looking down at the photo - we're sitting apart
With our eyes on each other - just joined at the heart.
Afraid to be seen holding hands, by our peers,
Afraid of their scorn, and their laughter and jeers.
Pressure from parents who thought us too young,
Our love was a melody - lyrics unsung.
We hid in the park - hoped we wouldn't be found,
Never had love been more deep and profound.
As the sun ran its course through the blue summer sky,
We knew, in our hearts, we were saying 'Goodbye.'
Glancing through lashes, eyes brimming with pain,
We had to return to the real world again.
As I stare at the photo my eyes fill with tears,
Though the pain has now dulled with the passing of years.
One day, in my life, that I'll never forget,
A memory of heaven, with a tinge of regret.
How I wish I'd had courage to ask you to stay,
How I wish I had held you and loved you that day.
Oh Kevin, the memory has sweetened with time,
Of that day, in the park, when I knew you were mine.

J Clarke

DON'T FORGET THIS CHRISTMAS
(Dedicated to Jackie Jackson, my lovely first wife
who died from breast cancer March 1995)

Hello, is that heaven? What? Oh, yes . . .
I've already given her name and the date of her death.
What's that? She's not allowed to talk to me,
But, I've got through, it's Christmas, please, can't you see
If rules can be waived, just this one time
The sound of her voice would make this Christmas shine.
Pardon? Oh yes you can confirm she's well and bright
And say she'll be thinking of us this Christmas night,
And sends her love, as strong as before.
Well, please give her mine, and tell her what's more
We all down here think of her each day
Although she's not here with us, she never goes away.
The line's fading . . . what's that . . . oh you say it's time to go
Well please wish her 'Merry Christmas, we all love you so.'

Mike Jackson

HIRAETH
(Dedicated to my grandparents, Grace and Herbert Weedon)

I see you in flowers,
When spring lambs speak with first voice
I hear your
Songs too, as there was always music
Always laughter, with you
I see you in my mother
I'll see you in my children
You echo in Welsh mountains
In fjords of Norway
Over Venetian skies
In Africa your stories poured from my heart
You are colours
When the hand of autumn touches
On a morning dressed in milky pearl
An amethyst jewelled night
I speak of you with words of fond love
There are parts of you in me
Your guidance will always be mine
When I long for you
You are everywhere.

Hazel Houldey

DEDICATION

Who is that man in the swivel chair
With his understanding ways, his kindly stare
Caring and empathy to me he's shown
At times when I've felt very low and alone
Always trying to put me at ease
Giving his time and patience to please
And make me feel better once more
I know with him I can be sure
Whatever I tell him I know it will be
In the strictest confidentiality
So who is this man that I write about
That I trust with my life there is no doubt
He's my doctor of course who else could it be
I've got the best lucky old me.

Anita Barnes

REUNITED

(Dedicated to Karen)

Sweet innocent, conceived in sin,
When I was but myself a child,
Was stupid, ignorant of sex,
Then by my family was reviled.
You didn't ask for life, or love,
In shame and anguish you were born
To me, who helpless, homeless and bereft,
Could raise no fight as from me you were torn.

Adoption - such a fearsome word.
So final, thus the bond was broken.
The tears, the heartache long endured,
No message passed, no words were spoken.
So many years in misery,
The separation caused such pain,
As bad for you as it was for me,
Until at last we met again.

The tears, the accusations flew -
How could you give your child away?
Because I'd nought to offer you,
They had it all, is what I say.
Recriminations, anger, hate,
Through all these spectra we have come,
To gain respect and, at last, love,
Now our relationship's begun.

Pauline Hepple

MY BROTHER JOHN

My brother, it was from our mother's womb that made our
Lives entwine
Even though we lived for years apart,
We both grew like a healthy vine.
Through the years although we did not know it,
We followed similar tasks
Whilst we kept up our happy masks.
We both loved photography, elephants, tigers
Plus the Red Indian tribes
Both of us indulged ourselves in these happy vibes
Even our taste was the same in culture and music too
Now we know it was from our mother our love of poetry grew.
Even our choice in food was the same
And when we feel unwell our enjoyment of life does wane.
Although 20 years separate this sister from her brother
When we finally met again, it was like looking in the
Mirror at the other.
It's so easy for us to relax and share our time
Because our thoughts are the same, including our ability to rhyme.
We are together soul mates, friends as well as that blood tie
That's why we understand each other when we want to cry.
If I was to lose again this brother and my friend
What would life have to hold for me until my end?

Jean Rendell

FAMILY THOUGHTS AT CHRISTMAS

As Christmas approaches I think once again
Of those I have loved and how many remain
Of loved ones lost in that time swirling mist
So many have died, that I know, from that list

There are some who I feel may be out there
Perhaps in a world much too busy to share
Alive somewhere, maybe, with thoughts just of me?
Or perhaps old age has lost memory's key?

I wish I could show and instil in each mind
That there is still family for them to find
That I am here waiting to share their strife
Someone they have known since my mum gave me life

Someone whose memory can't leave them behind
(Filled with life and youth and foreheads unlined)
Who thinks constantly how we were once so close
(When one was sad we all had tears lachrymose)

We all ganged together to fight just for one
(We didn't stop until that trouble was done)
And then we all parted to follow one's path
Which I'm regretting in this sad aftermath

Of those who are left I would wish once again
That once more we could gather and so obtain,
Though reduced in number, that closeness once more
That I so remember behind one front door

Royston E Herbert

'E'ASY ENJOYMENT

This poem is to be read by anyone
who has tried drugs before, for a bit of 'fun',
It's about my friend, he once tried them,
but he never will again.
Lying in the hospital bed,
not knowing if soon he might be dead.

All those drips and tubes and all,
machines bleeping on the wall.
His eyes are heavy, his face is white,
will my friend be alright?
Last night he was out until late,
partying with his so-called mates.

His friends stopped dancing, called over his mates,
offered them Ecstasy at a good rate.
His friend said: 'Buy it to have a good time,
it's only E, what's the crime?
If you want to be 'in', and have fun,
just take this, then it's done.'

It was peer pressure my friend gave into,
what else could he say? What else could he do?
He had started sweating and couldn't breathe,
his friends saw him like this, and decided to leave.
My friend had thrown a fit on the floor,
it turns out his tablet wasn't pure.

This means you could overdose on one little pill,
making my friend unconscious and seriously ill.
The machines gives out one long bleep,
my friend will never wake up from his sleep.
Please think twice about taking Ecstasy,
don't make your family suffer, like my friend did to me.

Janice Tucker

MICHAEL

If I couldn't touch him
Or hold him close to me,
My life would have no meaning,
My dreams would not be free.

My reason for existing
Would disappear from sight,
To leave a vacant presence,
A dying flame of light.

If I'd never met him
Or found his soothing smile,
My path would be uncertain
Without his certain style.

He sweeps away my darkness
Encased within his arms,
Provides a blend of comfort
Found deep inside his charms.

If the Wheel of Fortune
Had stopped before my time,
I'd have lost a dear companion,
A special friend of mine.

There'd be no morning sunrise
No music in the air,
There'd be no time to listen,
If Michael wasn't there.

Josephine Duthie

FRIENDSHIP'S TRIBUTE: TO BC

Amid life's harassments and complex cares
We crave the comfort of a loyal friend,
So lucky if that fond companion shares
Old memories that the present hour transcend.

One such I know - and you I celebrate,
Your loving nature and your noble mind,
Forgiving, courteous, and with trust so great
As in this changing world we'd hope to find.

And so my heart lifts when you come in view:
Your pointed ears and lovely thoughtful face,
Your furry paws and eyes of deepest blue,
Your cheering purr all strains and stresses chase.

Then as you drape yourself across my chest,
We tell each other just how much we're blest.

Anne Sanderson

A FRIEND IN NEED

I'm writing in your Christmas card -
It doesn't seem enough
Only to put a 'To' and 'From',
And 'Happy Xmas' stuff.

It's hard to seal my meaning
In a message from the heart,
But time slips by so quickly,
I suppose I'd better start.

Thank you for being there for me
When everything looked grey -
Health and hope and family
Shattered, or gone astray.

Your smile was gently cheering
When I looked into your face -
The sun shone brightly, peering in
To see our fond embrace.

And still it shines as warmly
From a sky now kindly blue,
Distance can never wipe away
My memories of you.

Beryl M Smith

BRIGHT LIVES

I should have left this town
A long time ago
Friends I had passed away
Permanently
A long time ago
Leaving nothing but memories and
Worries which do not show
Now there is nothing left except
Blank footsteps in the snow
Tunes on records and CDs
Which I remember from
Bright lives
Bright days
Bright friends
Bright years ago.

Ted Gibson

THE JOGGER'S FRIEND
(Dedicated to all non-joggers, everywhere)

I don't like jogging much; do you?
I think I'd rather have the flu.
At least, then, just my nose would run -
Although 'snot nice, 'twould be more fun.

I don't like jogging, as I said;
In fact, I'd rather stay in bed.
Which I could, if I had the flu -
And I'd be safe from traffic, too.

I don't like jogging. Fair enough.
I'm always running out of puff.
We really are an unfit nation.
Ah, here's my friend - the . . .
                                        railway station!

Roger Williams

MUM'S THE WORD

A mother's life's not easy
So often put to test,
She worries over family
And tries to do her best,
And even when she's tired
Has had a busy day,
A mother just gets on with it,
It is a mother's way.

Dear mother let me tell you
I love you very much,
There's none that could replace you
Your voice, your smile, your touch,
And even when I've hurt you
You've always been right there,
To back me up and help me
To show me that you care.

As Christmas time approaches
It's my turn now to say,
I wish you joy and happiness
In every kind of way.
I'll do my best to mirror
The love you've given me,
Best wishes, Happy Christmas
From all your family.

Irene Carter

To Kim

I'm going to be a Grandad,
You could say I'm excited,
I'm overjoyed, delighted,
And all because of you.

I'm going to be a Grandad,
And Mum will be a Grandma,
Our lives will have a new star,
To shine, because of you.

I'm going to be a Grandad,
I want to shout it out loud,
I feel so pleased, I'm so proud,
To say, because of you.

I'm going to be a Grandad,
Dear daughter, you'll be Mummy,
That sounds a little funny,
But true, because of you.

I'm going to be a Grandad,
I'm so full of elation,
A brand new generation,
Begun, because of you.

I'm going to be a Grandad,
What makes you think I'm happy?
Can't wait to change a nappy,
Maybe - Because of you.

I'm going to be a Grandad,
I know I'm very lucky,
'Cos if the nappy's mucky,
I'll hand it back to you!

Jim Sargant

DEAR BROTHER

Do you remember
when we were kids
of Christmas Past
and the things we did?
Creeping downstairs
when we should have been asleep
just to take a crafty peek.

The Christmas tree
with the fairy on top.
The chocolate pennies
we loved a lot.
We'd sit by the fireside
our faces aglow.
Unwrapping our presents
the joy we did know.

Eating Brazil nuts, and walnuts
and chestnuts too.
Going to see Grandma
were the things we would do.
Fond memories of the sixties
a long time ago.
but they don't fade or tarnish
I just wanted you to know.
So merry Christmas dear brother
for the best years of all.

Denise Hemingway

FEELINGS - WORDS UNSAID

*(I have dedicated this poem to my mum, Yasmin Suraiyya
I will always love you)*

365 days in a year, and I can never
find a moment to tell you this . . .
so I am taking a moment now mum to
say this . . .
You've had dreams, put on hold, dreams
that have never come true, but you've never
given up.
You've never had an exciting career
or beautiful clothes.
You've never had a fancy car or
travelled the world.
All this, plus many other things are
being put on hold . . . all because . . .
Every day you look after me, worry
about me, feed me, love me and care
about me, all without expecting anything
in return.
You've given two lives -
My own and yours.

Aysha Rubeena Suraiyya (12)

LIGHT OF MY LIFE
(For Jean)

You will always be the light of my life
When I asked you one day to be my wife
So many hours we have spent together
You will always remain in my heart forever.

Light of my life the only one for me
Together forever it wasn't meant to be
I'm all alone now so sad and lonely
But you my love remain the one and only

It doesn't seem such a long time ago,
That we were together then you had to go
But fear not my dear, I'll be there, I'll be slow
And in your loving arms I will be once more.

So please wait for me just be patient and strong
Every second, every minute is ever so long
And when I reach you, will you then be my wife
For you my Jean, you are the light of my life.

Graham Macnab

DEDICATION TO A NIECE

All my nieces and nephews are very dear to me,
Especially one niece.
As far as I know she is unaware of this,
As I wished to keep the peace.

I've watched her grow from babyhood,
Into those work-worn days,
But come what may she never lost
Her kind and loving ways.

She climbed to the top of her profession,
Not the easy way.
She had decided higher education wasn't for her you see
So she learnt the art of dealing with all by being apprenticed by the day.

She now has a little family of her own,
And lovely children they be.
Into all things just like Mum and Dad,
Ask any of them what they would like of life,
The answer's usually, 'Just you wait and see . . .'

Betty Green

THE CULTIVATORS

(In memory of Alex Gibson (founder of Dalry Art Club)
Ross Stevenson and Alistair Dunn)

Fond memories of these three
Who did not look down on me
From their great height
Who showed me colour through
An artist's eye
Replacing my vision of black and white.

Thanking them for criticism constructive
Calling a spade a spade
Never in any way destructive
Showing me where to dig

Then planting seeds of praise
Upon my unearthed talent
That fertilised by their encouragement
Came to flower in the sale of my
first painting.

Heather Kirkpatrick

GRANDSON
(Dedicated to a special Grandson)

Hello dear Grandson! Take my hand,
Through life we'll go along
To find the paths of happiness,
Sing many a favourite song.
When on those sturdy legs you'll run,
Or climb among the heather,
We'll watch the wild and nesting birds
But will disturb them never.
I hope like me you'll love the hills
And snow-capped mountains high,
The magic of all nature's scenes
Like pine trees pointing to the sky.
Grow strong and wise beside your mother,
Dear child, be blessed as she
Who'll teach and guide you through the years
Until a man of worth you'll be.

Sylvia Taggart

SEPARATION

'Will you ever forget?'

Will I ever forget the one who touched me so gently,
who in one brief moment turned my conveyor belt existence
into something alive?

'Will you ever forget?'

How could I possibly forget the one whose presence
fills me with light and life, whose thread but brushed against mine,
yet in that smallest of moments instilled me with a tenderness
that I will feel until the end of my days?

'Will you ever forget?'

To you, my heart, I can make this promise -
I can speak this phrase, this jumble of letters,
and, maybe for the first time, I can fully understand its meaning.

'Will you ever forget?'

I will *never* forget.

Pedro Wrobel

FOR MARGARET

Although you've moved quite far away,
Our thoughts are with you every day,
Dearest Margaret, sister, friend,
Just for you these thoughts are penned.

We wish you peace in dwelling new,
May aims be high, displeasures few,
Your choice of habitat is grand,
Maybe with glimpse of softest sand.

Perchance you'll think of Devon tors,
The glorious land that once was yours,
Yet Sussex is a handsome place,
It's sweeping downs your feet to pace.

The festive season now draws near,
When we remember those held dear,
So all the best to Margaret kind,
Forever in our hearts entwined.

Ann Madge

BORN ON THE 25TH DECEMBER

So close and yet so far away -
Twenty years ago on this very same day,
I was rushed to a hospital not far away -
Then two hours later in my arms you lay!

So close and yet so far away,
For your phone call home, I'll be waiting all day,
When it comes there's just so much to say,
But oh how I'll miss you on Christmas Day!

So close and yet so far away,
Helping 'Hurricane Homeless', day after day.
I miss you but my heart is full of pride,
I'm so proud of you - they too might have died!

Cindy White

A LETTER TO HEAVEN
(Dedicated to my mum)

A Christmas card I would send to my mum,
I would send it to Heaven via the holy angels,
My message would read, 'I think of you everyday and miss you.'
It has been a hard two years as you sent no word of goodbye.
So unexpected and sudden life was very cruel,
My heart is always full of sadness
If I could reach you by telephone how nice that would be
To hear your voice, we could chat for ages that would be wonderful
I would say, 'Merry Christmas.'
Every day you are in our thoughts
We would send so many kisses and lots of hugs
My message is only short, but it is dedicated to a special *mum*
God's garden must be beautiful as it holds my beautiful mum.
Sweet dreams. I love you so much.

Lynda E Schoepp

UNTITLED

When we were young we were a team,
Growing up together to our early teens.
Born a year apart there were no others
To share the love we had for each other.

We argued, we fought
We cried together,
Sharing a love
That would last forever.

The years rolled on
The time flew by
You went your way,
I went mine.

You now live across the sea,
Far away from me it seems,
Now I see you but once a year,
Not enough for me I feel.
But you my dearest sister Jill
Are in my heart eternally.

Pattie Lopez

A TRIBUTE TO MY DAUGHTER

God blessed us forty years ago by sending you to us,
Your brothers were excited too and created quite a fuss.

'A little sister come at last,' they said, and loved you very much,
Your mum and dad held you so close with such a gentle touch.

The years have passed, we've been so proud of all the things you've
                                                                    done
And kindness to each one you've met, whose hearts you've always
                                                                    won.

Your brothers living miles away, you're all so far apart,
But though not close in distance I'm sure you're in their heart.

For me, your loving mum, you're a precious part of life
Who's there for me through happiness, who helps me through the strife.

Your dad, he had to leave us, without a choice to stay.
He loved you so, dear daughter, in a very special way.

I do not need to tell you what a rock you've been for me,
The care you give to all of us is very plain to see.

God bless you now and always, don't ever change my dear
And when I have to leave you, like your dad, I'll still be near.

Frieda Cox

ODE TO DOROTHY

Dorothy was a special friend
In many, many ways
Her strength, vitality, thoughtfulness
Brightened up my days.
Her cheery voice upon the phone
The way she said, 'Hello ooo'
I can't believe she's not around
I'm sure she is you know.

We used to meet for coffee
And chats with all our friends
The laughter, the discussions
And news of family trends.
We sometimes went to dancing
Scottish Reels or slow Strathspey's
Or sometimes for a coach trip to a city or a town
Sometimes we just talked
About whatever came around.

She'd telephone to tell me
Of a party or the theatre
Ask if I would like to go
And join her later.
She'd tell of all the news
Of what was going on in church
And this little ode is just to say
I miss her very much.

She told me of the fashion show
Upon that fateful night
And even gave a ticket
To be sure I came alright.
It was the last I ever saw her
As her spirit flew away
She left behind these memories
'Cause we'll meet again one day.

Jean Ferguson

MY SON

You're far away
But not forgotten,
You're not with me
Except in my heart,
I can't see you
But in my mind's eye,
So in truth
We never part.

V G Walker

FOR ADRIENNE . . .

For your face is like an angel,
For your hands I give you dreams,
For your feet I give the whole world,
To find out what it means.

For your mind I'll give you guidance,
For your heart I'll give support,
For your eyes there is so much to see,
Your mouth is to report.

For you I'll give a perfect love
Purer than any other
For you, you are my miracle
And I, I am your mother.

Kathryn Forrest

THE GHOST OF CHRISTMAS PAST
(For Dad, died August 1981. God bless)

I'm sitting in that well-loved room.
We sat here long ago,
surrounded by your records, books,
your maps and stereo.

I've packed up all your things with care,
and put mine out instead.
I cannot play your records now;
your books remain unread.

The music is too poignant, and
the books hold memories
of Christmases when, more often than not,
we would just sit silently

joined by a love of Beethoven,
of Shakespeare, Wordsworth, Keats
of Mozart, Haydn, Handel, Bach,
of De la Mare and Yeats.

We'd communicate through others' words,
their dreams, philosophies.
We didn't talk about our own,
nor recall memories.

But when you died, I came down here,
and looked at what you'd left.
I saw my childhood fade from sight
in adulthood bereft.

And though I never said as much,
I loved you, even so -
the father who shared those Christmases
of childhood long ago.

J M Service

MY BENJI

I went to the woods today,
But Lady didn't want to play.
You see, we miss your company
But in my heart you'll always be,
My Benji.

I miss you lying at my feet,
I miss you when it's time to eat.
I miss you barking when I'm hanging out the washing
It was these times that made you,
My Benji.

You were my handsome beast,
My chocolate boy who loved a feast.
My comfort when I was sad,
My joy when I was glad.
You are my Benji

And now there is only Lady and me,
You had to leave us, but maybe
If it be God's will,
I may see you again still
But you'll always be my Benji.

Rose Baines

DEDICATED TO SHARON

I've always wanted God to send,
To me a very special friend.
The moment you came through the door,
I knew I need to ask no more.

Louise Everitt

FOREVER

(Dedicated to Graham. My love, my hope, my inspiration)

We've walked the rocky road of life,
From teenage love to man and wife,
Through sorrow . . . many tears we've cried,
But we've come through it, side by side.

You are my everlasting tower of strength,
Not just my husband but my best friend,
When it comes to facing my greatest fears,
Your loving arms are always near.

The special love we feel for each other,
Has overflowed and created two others,
With a son and a daughter we are blessed,
As a father you truly are the best.

Our love has withstood the test of time,
I will always by yours, you will always be mine,
In the years that are left we will face life together,
Our love wild last forever and ever!

Tracy Bell

I HAVE HAD A GLIMPSE OF PARADISE
(To AP)

I have walked under skies of
blue and bathed in seas
of crystal azure whose
colours defy even an artist's pallet
and make the poets weep.

I have walked up mountains
and felt the gentle rain
falling as angels' tears
which fall because of
the sheer beauty of it.

I have seen stars as jewels
mounted with loving precision
upon a ceiling of velvet black
receding only upon
dawn's silent return.

I have felt your warmth
and touched your soft
peach-like body in my
own private awakening
strengthening me for the
treacherous hours that lie ahead.

Such paradise was too much
for one so lowly
you have gone and with
you the paradise I so long for .

will it ever return
will those hours
again be captured
and will we see yet
another dawn together?

Paul Elwell

KEEPING IN TOUCH

Honestly, I have been meaning to write,
But somehow the timing was never quite right.
And I once did think of giving you a call,
Then didn't get round to phoning after all.
Spare you details of terrible year it's been,
Our children, who had left home, now moved back in.
And on the health front, we have all been quite ill,
My husband is still taking a course of pills.
But on a lighter note while it's on my mind,
I do hope you all have a great Christmastime.

Susan Mullinger

TO MY LOVED ONE

(This poem is to my loved one)

Dear loved one,

I'm writing this to you
But I'm not sure what to say
Then that doesn't really matter
You don't know it's for you anyway.

You don't know that I love you
You don't know that I care
You don't know how much it hurts me
To know that she is there.

You never see me cry at night
You never see me weep
You'll never know the pain I feel
Or this secret that I keep.

Until the day that she is me
You won't know that he is you
This poem is for my loved one
And only I know that is you.

Rachel Ritchie

MY MUM

Wherever I go in this life
Whatever I may do
I feel your spirit close to me
To help and guide me through

Whenever I softly call your name
To help heal my broken heart
I know that you are listening
And that we are never truly apart

Whenever I feel lonely
I'll try not to grieve or cry
Because I know in my heart
That you are still there for me
We will *never* say goodbye

Roger Lett

REMEMBER ME

You do not see me watching you,
My face hard-kissed by cold Jack Frost,
I'm hardly recognisable now,
I once had all, now all is lost.
The house which I once called my home,
Your smiles, your love, your Christmas cheer,
I have no right to claim as mine,
Now you are there and I am here.
I do not ask to be welcomed back,
I know I am no longer a part,
I only ask please think of me;
And remember me within your heart.

Andrea Kiernan

A MORE ENDURING HURT

She sits alone, staring through your thoughts again,
Do you remember the time when you knew her name
You're miles away from her eyes now,
Cold as the statue that comforts her,
Insecure as the blackness that shrouds her.
These walls might as well be blank.
Happy memories turn bloody sour,
More poison, more pain with every thinking hour.
A more enduring hurt than you'll ever know.
Why does she let you do this to her?
Why do you let her remind you?
Maybe you cared, but no love, - never love!
Never make yourself that vulnerable,
Or you'll end up as pathetic as her.

Helen Hill

READY, WILLING - EH, BILL?

My darling Bill, when first we met, you lured me with your charms,
then in a flash (with great panache)
ensnared me in your arms!
Our mutual love grew fast and strong - we very soon were wed
and five sons were enjoyably conceived
on bonk-stressed bed.

You proved to be a perfect Dad who doted on our mob,
'Enough, though, is enough,' said I,
'You've proved you know your job!'
You worked hard to provide for us, but back-pain took its toll
and - all too soon - heart valve disease
assumed a major role.

Then I sank, too, depressed and sick . . . you dragged me from the deep
and helped restore my will to live
when I could only weep.
Your heart now beats with plastic valve but, though it's working fine,
Fate's fickle finger often prods
another warning sign.

Yet never once do you complain, nor let self-pity rule -
you face up to adversity . . .
still acting like a fool!
Through ups and downs that life contrived, you steered our

family through
until, with five sons grown and flown,
we're back to me and you.

So, on we journey . . . me - in front, you - taking up the rear . . .
in wagon train formation
with powered chairs to steer
and, though we're fat and ageing, with hair streaked silver-grey,
you've been my zany, precious love
since that red-letter day.

Maureen Atkin

A CHRISTMAS MESSAGE TO MY DEAD WIFE

When I'm alone the tears flow
And sadness invades my heart;
Your passing leaves a void
That never will be bridged
And flowing years will never
Remove the memory of your presence . . .

A bright comet has illuminated my life
And with its passing there is much sorrow:
But to have walked through life with you
Has been a most enjoyable pleasure.

Arthur Pickles

LETTER TO MY SON

Dearest,

   I could say . . .
It is raining, or it is not raining.
I am better now, perhaps a little tired.
I have read a poem, or dreamed a dream.
It is January, not June, and the
steely grey skies are still and quiet.
And such conventional exchanges
are of no consequence . . . can neither
harm or heal.

Yet,
Child of my Heart,
simply, my wish is to convey
my continual awareness
of your absence.

Louise Rogers

COMMUNICATION
(To my daughter)

Thirteen thousand mils away,
So distant on Christmas day.
But not so far by telephone
New Zealand seems much nearer home.

Greetings over, news begins
Big events, so many things
To ask, to question and to hear
My daughter's world we hold so dear.

She said she had lunched today
On boiled ham and cold turkey.
Christmas pudding was far too hot,
And on the beach, she thought not.

Her children played in the sea
Running in and out with glee.
The sun had shone with fiery glow
Baking the sand and shells below.

My daughter misses so much
Our winter snow and cold touch
Of frosty mornings white with rime,
She hasn't seen for such a time.

Told her we had rain today,
Of her nieces come to play.
And of some old friends dropping by
For good cheer and Christmas pie.

The phone bill is growing fast
As the minutes quickly pass.
We say goodbye, hang up the phone
New Zealand now seems far from home.

Isobel M MacLarnon

MOTIVATION

It isn't that I love you more, my dear
As Christmas time approaches;
I am sure you understand, all year,
Despite pitfalls, reproaches,
My strong affection for you never dies,
It may waver like a flame
But endures - you must read it in my eyes,
Hear it when I speak your name.
You see, when all things seem to scintillate
And when fingers intertwine
And, more than ever, loving seems so great
A thing, I thrill that you're mine.
I need to throw my arms about you tight
As part of this atmosphere
And loneliness seems even more a blight,
Vacuous without you near.
Espying multi-coloured candles blaze
Festive decorations lure;
I need to share with you these blissful days
And part-living, wait, endure.
When eagerly I hear your vibrant voice,
Realise you're living too, no myth but true,
It's Christmas time for real - I can rejoice;
I do not hold unfeeling phone - but you!

Ruth Daviat

LET ME COUNT THE WAYS I LOVE THEE ...
ONE ...
(For John)

In words I express the inner thoughts I feel
But in those that I speak
You sometimes get a raw deal
So pen to pad I write to you
Simply more than I love you
But as I try it's hard to share
To get those words of which I despair
To explain how much you mean to me
Beyond those words, you know which three
But there is much more
That I want to say
But I never do any day
But nevertheless they are here in my heart
Whether we are together or even apart
So I hope you will let me dedicate this writing to you
For no matter whatever,
    I always love you.

Maria Waters

THROUGH TIME AND SPACE TO YOU . . .

My first Noel without you.
Remembrance of years past,
Lying safe within your arms,
Watching shadows cast
Their changing shapes across the walls
Of cerulean blue.
Gold curtains closed against the dark,
The snow-strewn outer view.

A log fire wafts aromas
Of woods and glowing coal.
I came to you, with self in shreds.
Your loving made me whole.
With you, I face 'unfaceables'
At peace and psyche strong.
But this Christmas, my darling,
Home's *not* where you belong.

Your mother's dying worlds away.
You're flying to her side.
My spirit's there beside you.
'I'll be just fine!' I lied.

No indication yet as to
How long we'll be apart.
But when you're back we'll share a joyous
    Christmas of the heart.

Elizabeth Mark

HILLARY

The good angel,
not thinking this of himself:

sticking to the facts,
unassuming but not self-effacing,

putting up with adversity
from within, close by, wherever,

philosophical in his seventies
as he always was,

helping others, as himself,
in the normal, unobtrusive course;

among the bad angels,
an incorruptible example,

he touches many people
with an unspoken blessing

Neville Davis

THERE'S LIFE IN THE OLD DOG YET

I'd like to dedicate this rhyme
To my old faithful pet.
He's getting rather long in tooth,
But he ain't finished yet!

He stares at telly hours on end,
And growls at Gary Numan.
And watching Coronation Street
You'd think that he was human!

I think of him in days gone by,
When he was keen and quicker.
I've had him since he was a 'Babe'
A present from the Vicar.

Although he's slow and looks his age,
We're always found together.
We go out 'walkies' every day
In every wind and weather.

His bark is much worse than his bite,
His coat gets in a muddle,
And like old dogs about his age
He likes a kiss and cuddle!

And just in case you've got it wrong,
And think my Fred's a pup.
He often puts his paper down
And does the washing-up!

Peter Davies

Dedicated To: Flo
Our Beloved West Highland Terrier

I hope you are well, Flo. Since you went away the nights are much
longer, much longer than day.
The days are all soulless, all cloudy and grey. Do you know that we
miss you, since you went away?
The twelve years we knew you flew by in a trice. We thought we
had time to do everything twice
But that isn't true, Flo. Life isn't that nice. Each one of us lives by
the throw of a dice.
It's frosty outside now. The nights are so cold, as cold as my heart was
the day we were told
That you had a tumour and wouldn't grow old. Oh, how could we lose
you, more precious than gold?
A cure was suggested. Where fools fear to tread my family and I by
the doctors were led
But it just didn't work, Flo, and I held your head and three seconds later
we knew you were dead.
You were such a bright star, Flo, a brilliant young brain, the like of this
sad world will not see again.
Our cruel, lonely loss has been Heaven's good gain and, thank God, you
no longer have illness and pain.
What happened to you, Flo, will burn us for years. The fire's deep
inside us. Our memories it sears
But the flames won't be able to dry all our tears now we can't see your
face and we can't scratch your ears.
We look to the future, the future's all black. We wish we could have
our dear terrier back.

She was right in the centre, the boss of our pack but we've only her
ashes and a little brass plaque.
I'm thinking about her as I drink my tea. Our summers in Norfolk
and her in the sea!
She loved all the wavelets, our lives were so free. Though we'd like
to go back there it never can be.
So I raise my cup in salute even though my heart bleeds each time that
the knife is turned slow
But on some occasions my memory will glow and there she is, happy,
our beautiful *Flo.*

L S Robinson

SILLY QUARRELS (FAMILY)

Please will you wait a minute,
Don't throw this note away,
Please read this slow and carefully,
Please let me have my say.
We're not getting any younger,
Let's put aside the past,
We've had our ups and downs, I know,
Let's make a brand-new start.
For the sake of those who love us,
For the sake of those who care,
Please can we make an effort,
Discard the grudge we bear.
We've hurt each other badly,
What's done is done, it's true,
But beneath it all, we're Family,
And I really care for you.
So, please, will you wait a minute,
Don't throw this note away,
Let Peace be ours this Christmas,
And Friendship true to stay.

Pat Weeks Goodridge

TO MY PUPILS

Children I've known and cherished for so long:
Though I am old, and you have gone away,
Stay, stay in my heart and be my song.

Forgive me when I, heedless, did you wrong,
Found not the words you needed me to say . . .
Children I've known and cherished for so long.

The world of future is where you belong -
You must walk forward; yet I seem to pray:
Stay, stay in my heart and be my song.

May you be hopeful, growing true and strong,
Able to fight, and give (forgive!) - and play,
Children I've known and cherished for so long.

To find you all in heaven again, I long.
Till then, while each of you go your different way,
Stay, stay in my heart and be my song.

Together, shy or bold, we came along
The path that's led us to each new today.
Children I've known and cherished for so long:
Stay, stay in my heart and be my song.

Katharine Holmstrom

THE VISITOR

Here we go again!
You're moving things around,
Knocking on my bedroom door
Sometimes much too loud!
I turn lights off . . .
You switch them on . . .
You tap me on your way.
We see you all too briefly
When you come to stay.
Having playful tendencies
Causes no alarm
And scent so pure and beautiful
Is comforting and warm.
You visit for a reason,
Belief, I have, will stay,
Of reassuring guidance
Along Life's motorway.

Caroline J Sammout

DEDICATION

May the bluebird of happiness,
Always fly with you,
To bring you love, joy and fulfilment.
And may the elephant of good fortune,
Guide you along life's highway,
To ensure you will always,
Have reason to rejoice,
In life's many blessings.

Gerry Boxall

MARK, MY WORDS

Gray eyes, entice, or plead, all that is Mark,
soft shadows lie by darkness in that smile,
he took my hand and led me from the dark.
No lies, pretence, ignites the dying spark,
warm skin to bring real pleasure all the while,
gray eyes entice or plead all that is Mark,
sweet scent, the forest green, ripe fruit, aged bark,
bright matchless flame illuminates cold guile,
he took my hand and led from the dark,
set free, for laughter echoes shall I hark,
deny myself what cannot bear denial,
gray eyes entice or plead, all that is Mark,
soft shadows lie by darkness in that smile.

Hyd

DEDICATED TO . . .

Dedicated to
You for being there when I needed you most,
listening when I so needed someone to talk to.
Dedicated to
Him for making us meet in the first place,
and then allowing our friendship to blossom.
Dedicated to
You for showing me what it is to hurt.
Dedicated to
Her for hurting me and leading me to the strong person I am now.
Dedicated to
Him for shaping me both mentally and physically and looking
after me every day,
Dedicated to
You for being my friend and my sister,
Dedicated to
Him for showing me love and giving me all those things
I always took for granted.
Dedicated to
You for caring about me
Dedicated to
Him for making me what I am and guiding me through
each day.

K Navsa (16)

MISSED

When I hear those Christmas carols,
Or feel the yuletide spirit,
As usual, I want to give it a miss,
Because I know you won't be coming,
Still I hang up my mistletoe,
But I have no one to kiss,
You won't be here for Christmas,
I face the festivities on my own,
The laughter and joy,
Left this house with you,
I pray every day that you will soon come home,
Christmas means little to me now,
I'd rather not bother at all,
But it's unavoidable, it's everywhere,
So for appearance's sake,
I hang my cards around the wall,
But emptiness fills my heart,
Especially on Christmas Day,
As I sit and sink into a bottle,
Day and night merge becoming a blur,
It's well into tomorrow that my telephone,
Forces me to stir,
But I'm far too late to speak,
No message was left, one four seven one,
Only told me in a monotonous tone,
Sorry the caller's number was withheld,
Sorry the caller's number was withheld,
So I sit and fritter away my days in the
                                    desperation zone.

P J Littlefield

TO MARY

Now is the time that I should write a card
To send my love and blessings for this Christmastide,
And thoughts and wishes for the coming year,
For happiness and health and more besides.

Now is the time that I should wrap your gifts
In coloured paper, red and gold and green
Bedecked with stars and golden angels, wings outstretched,
With coloured tags and bows and ribbons bright.

But you are gone - I can no longer write
To tell you that I love you still.
At the beginning of the year - suddenly -
No time to say goodbye, or thank you for the gifts you sent.

So I must think of Christmas in the past,
When we were children and the house was full of
Laughter, joy and warmth,
And music, happiness and love.

My thoughts are with you now, my heart is sad.
But when I sing the carols that we knew,
I'll sing for you, sweet sister mine,
With sadness and with love.

A Linney

DEDICATED TO MY DAUGHTER:
(A poem from her mother)

I give to you, my Daughter dear
This message for the coming year:

A calf observes her mother's ways,
Absorbing with her wide-eyed gaze
The ponderous movement through the day
And lazy groping on the way
For yet another snack of grass
Which doubly chewed will through her pass.
Above, the mild incurious stare
Will never question why or where
Or how to do things differently;
The calf looks on unthinkingly
And grows in height if not in grace,
Now well equipped to take her place.
What Mother did, the calf does now
She could not but become a Cow.

Yours, too, will be a fate as bland
If you don't take your life in hand.

Nicki Cornwell

TO MAM

On this special day
It gives me time to say
'Thank you Mam
For making me what I am.
Always being there,
When I need to share
Any exciting news
Or, when I am feeling blue.
Constantly staying in the background,
But most of all, loving me all year round.

Ida Dunwoodie

A MUM UNIQUE
(For Mary Moore)

It dawned on me
quite suddenly
what you have done
for everyone.

From what I see
automatically
you gave your life
as mum and wife.

With care and thought
you raised and taught
your family
and all for free!

With ups and downs,
occasional frowns
but *always* there;
a thing so rare.

With love unceasing,
time increasing,
so much attention
without a mention.

So I can speak
of a mum unique,
a special sort
that can't be bought.

We're miles apart
but from my heart
these words are few
Thank you, thank you.

Geraldine Moore

MIKE

December.
We walked on snow-covered fields.
We were hand-in-hand
Illuminated by the white expanse of sky.
I knew your secret heart
And how you'd given yourself
To the timeless journey.
Under our feet the lake ice
Held us between worlds,
Conscious of both, and without fear.
And that child-like abandon was never selfish,
But born out of a knowing
That once the heart centre was open
The true self would be revealed.

Linda Anne Landers

DEAR DAISY
(Written by another dog)

It's coming up to Christmas time,
And I thought I ought to drop a line,
It's months I haven't seen you,
I hope you miss me, I miss you too.

My family don't take me for long walks,
I just want to see you, have a talk,
I enjoy Christmas in many ways,
There's lots of food, a bone always.

But I can never run in the park,
By the time I get there it's always dark,
My owners never stop for ice-cream,
That cone we shared seems just a dream.

Remember when we shared that bone,
Just to think of it makes me feel alone,
I know we get into lots of trouble,
But I think we make the perfect couple.

So I am writing now at Christmas time,
To say Merry Christmas, that I'm feeling fine,
It's months I haven't seen you,
But the truth is, I still love you!

Anne Biggs (13)

FRIENDSHIP

Stand by - friend
Don't support me
Quietly allow me to change
What needs to be changed
Help me to accept the
Unchanging -
Your counsel is needed
For me to see
Between the two
My debt need not be your debt
Nor your debt mine
Stand by - friend
Back to back
Your firm quiet presence
Strengthens me alone.

Richard Stoker

MUM!
(I dedicate this poem to my mum)

My mum embarasses me
By doing silly things.
But when I'm sad
She cheers me up
So I don't really mind.

She takes me out
To different places
Where I like to go.
I love my mum
And she loves me.
She's wonderful
And kind to me.

Sara Fernandez (9)

DEDICATED

My mum helps me,
With my homework,
My mum is always there,
When I'm sad or alone,
My mum is always happy.

My dad is always there,
Although he is tired,
He plays some sport with
Me on Saturday,
My dad is always there.

My sister is always funny,
Even though she's unwell,
She laughs and plays all day,
I don't know what I'd do,
                    without her.

Kelly Webb (11)

I DEDICATE THIS POEM TO MY DAD

My dad is very funny,
Plays on computers all day,
He tells me funny jokes,
In every single way.

He takes me lots of places,
And makes me wash the car,
But he's OK sometimes,
Like when he gives me a chocolate bar.

Vicky Harbour (10)

BUGS BUNNY

Bugs Bunny you are so funny,
You walk around saying,
'What's up, Doc?'

No one can outsmart you,
For you're better than all the rest,
If you were in the second World War
You'd have the Germans all in
One blow.

You're top of the charts
With me.
If anyone else doesn't agree
I'll tell you,
Then sort them out,

Luke Brunt (10)

DEDICATED TO MICHAEL SCHUMACHER

I think you are good at driving,
And you are really cool,
I wish I was like you,
I know you were
A kart driver and so am I,
I want to be
An F1 driver like you.

Sam Hutchins (10)

DEDICATED TO MY DOG

My dog's name is Spike
He chews all the pipes
He plays with my ball
And he acts like a fool
He tries to eat my hamster
When he's in his ball.

William Thirkettle

DEDICATED

Dedicated to my dog

Do you know what Christmas
is about?
Well, it's about giving and thinking
about other people.
Some of us get presents and do you
know why?
It's because Jesus was born.

Sophie Honzik (10)

DEDICATED TO MY MOTHER

When it's raining Mum always brings the sun,
When I'm upset she always cheers me up,
I want to do something for her but what?
Maybe when she's upset I could cheer her up.

Karen Symour (10)

DEDICATED TO NIK, OUR COACH

Whether it's cold or whether it's hot,
Whether it's raining or whether it's not,

Football, basketball, volleyball day,
Nik, our coach, turns up to play.

Champions of this, winners of that,
Must be Nik's lucky base hat.

He must have got it a long time ago,
How old is it Nik, we'd all like to know?

But what we really want to do,
Is give our grateful thanks to you.

From all the members of your clubs (5 & 6)
Especially Shane and Tony

MY DAD

My dad lives far from me,
Sometimes he takes me out for tea,
He has brown hair and eyes,
And never tells any lies.
On a ferry is where he works,
And once he took me to see some fireworks.
Swimming is what I like best of all,
'Cause he throws me like a bouncy ball,
In the water with a splash.
It's just a shame he must always dash
As my family are separated,
But it still means I'm still related
                              to my dad.

Lewanné Müdd (10)

DEDICATED TO MY TEACHER

I have had the nicest week
in the month I have been
welcomed into this class
in a very nice way.

When I was waiting to come
to this school, I was very pleased.
I was like a pop group with
a single coming out.

I like it here.
I'll never move again.

Chloe Reed (9)

I DEDICATE THIS POEM TO MY DAD

My dad likes driving,
He drives quite fast.
He likes to think
He's racing against
Someone else.
He thinks he always wins.

Jonathan Wilcox (10)

I DEDICATE THIS POEM TO MY MUM

My mum is sweet,
She always helps me,
I like her smiles,
In great big piles.
She never lets me down
When she's not around.

Tara Godden (10)

DEDICATED TO THE WHITE FAMILY

The White family is so fine,
Especially when they are drinking wine,
The White family is so great,
So now let us all celebrate.
My mum is cool,
My dad is fun,
My brother is stupid,
And I am dumb.

Simon White (10)

DEDICATED TO MY CAT

My cat Sammy boy
Is soft as a rose,
He has long whiskers
And a cute pink nose,
My cat Sammy boy
Has very sharp claws,
A swishy grey tail,
With soft little paws.

My cat Sammy boy
Is just so clever,
I really must say
He's the best ever,
I wrote about him
To a magazine,
And then, yes, I won
You know what I mean?

Samantha Bryant (10)

ALAN SHEARER

I would like to dedicate
this poem to Alan Shearer

Alan Shearer, you're the best,
When I see you in your vest,

Number nine on your back,
Now you're looking for that gap,
The ball comes over, it's at your feet,
Only one defender to beat.

The crowd let out a massive cry,
You kicked the ball and let it fly.
The ball flew true, straight in the net,
What a goal, you bet!

Kirsty Cloke (11)

DEDICATED TO MY MUM

She takes care of me, ill or not,
Whatever happens she's always there,
If I'm upset we'll talk it through,
She helps me with my homework too,
I love my mum.

Danielle Edwards (11)

DEDICATED TO FIONA, MY WIFE

'You leave the place untidy with clothes strewn all around'
She says regularly with anger, and always stands her ground.

'You never come to town with me and take interest in what I've bought'
I'm sometimes quite intrigued, but often not a lot.

'You keep me wakened every night with your snoring in our bed'
Funny I never hear it - it must all be in her head.

'Your smoking might just kill you and leave the kids without a dad'
This point I must concede as it would end up very sad.

'At bedtime you're perverted with the things you try to do'
It's just a healthy sexual appetite - always keen on something new.

'You spend so much time at the office, you should sleep there every
night'
I'm trying to impress the bosses - some time they may see the light.

'The kids have been horrendous, it's your family side I see'
Only good things could come from *my* side of the family tree.

'The inside of the car is disgusting, why don't you ever clean it out'
'Why have a dog and bark yourself?' Is a phrase I often shout.

Although we have our differences, towards her grow and grow
And the extent that I love her is too much for her to know.

Christopher Leith

Country Gal

A little lady, who comes over, big,
With a gorgeous body, and a blonde wig,
Queen of the Grand Old Oprey,
Way down in Nashville, Tennessee.

You have given us, so much pleasure,
A real southern, national treasure,
Has dueted, with the world's best,
Real bundle of dynamite, works without rest.

Many hits, across the land,
Written by your own special hand,
Songs of love and pain, and regret,
So many to remember, none you forget.

Progressed from music, to the silver screen,
Nine to five, salt in my tears, and Jolene,
Has this wonderful Texan drawl,
Honey, we sure do, love you all.

Who is also in, the hall of fame,
So far, I have not given her name,
Has started, our weekly lottery,
The one and only, Dolly P.

Robert Thompson

MY CHRISTMAS DEDICATION

It will be another happy Christmas, spent with both of you
Such a wonderful couple, without you what would I do?
You'll make it really special, we'll have a lot of fun
I really am so lucky to have a good kind Stepdad and Mum

You always think of everything, no expense will you spare
Christmas delicacies to eat and drink, for me to come and share
Carefully chosen presents, all wrapped so prettily
Surprise gifts that we long for, placed round the Christmas tree

I accept your kind invitation, I can't wait to come and stay
To reminisce of many a past Christmas or all the games we play
To relax in front of the log fire, with a glass of wine
Watching TV or just talking, a really happy time

Not only at Christmas but every day all year through
All the things you do for me, I say a big thank you
You both are really dear to me, I truly love and care
I can't imagine what it would be like, if neither of you were there

I have many treasured memories, that really makes me glad
I will always be able to remember the happy times we had
I know that I am fortunate, I know that I have been blessed
To be able to call you my family, you simply are the best

Linda Brown

STEVE'S POEM

Steve I love you,
You bring happiness to my heart
You are my friend and my kindred spirit,
and you are my other half.
You are very kind hearted,
Fun and gentle too, intelligent and sensitive,
I know your love is true.
We met, we touched, we kissed,
It seemed soon, but right,
The way you held me,
The way you loved me,
The passion of that first night.
I love you in so many ways,
You are so much part of me.
I hope one day soon, we will live
                    together happily.
My love for you never changes,
You are my light, my heart, my soul,
My knight, my guardian angel,
To save me from life's black hole!
So when at night you lie awake,
Say a prayer, before you sleep,
That God will keep you safe,
And I shall make your life complete.

Jane M Turney

DEDICATED TO MY THREE DEAR CHILDREN (NOW GROWN UP)

My children three
Stephen, Simon and Suseé,
Are the whole wide world to me
They are my love, my life, my very being!

They are kind and thoughtful, loving and giving
Caring and sharing, making life worth living,
I am so lucky to have them,
And give thanks each day
For being their mum in every way!

Now I have another 'daughter' (in-law) Diane,
So dainty and neat,
Capable and thoughtful,
And very sweet!

The time has now come,
A Grandma they have made me
With two gorgeous little girls - Lisa and Hollié
As cuddly as can be!

Edna Parrington

MY DEAR DAD

Although you're out of this world and into the next,
If I could pay you a tribute, this would be my text.

You are and always will be my unseen escort,
Your wisdom I use daily, so learned but self-taught,
Fine common sense enfolds me as home-spun enriching cloak,
Word-painter of life for kin to use and share with other folk.

Look up and never look down,
Or furrow brow into a frown,
Question! Frowning is utter turn down,
Watch, heed, to achieve life's black gown.

Do not join the spilled milk ilk,
Confront your problems, never bilk,
Life can be remains as buttermilk
Or smooth the curd to feel like silk.

Eyes front and never look back,
Blitzing yourself with needless flak,
Leastways, causing detour or side-track,
Else becoming insomniac.

Without flexibility
To adapting ability
You will miss an opportunity
If you inject immunity.

Victors stride uphill, onward,
Far-reaching, far-sighted, forward,
Take direct route, journey straight forward,
Waverers roam wayward homeward.

Remember! If coming first doesn't manifest,
You'll be a winner if you've tried your best,
Not the end of the world, a preparatory test
To do our utmost for good while here as God's guest.

Hilary Jill Robson

FOREVER (WE'LL BE)

Roses, snowdrops, daffodils too
Beautiful scents that remind me of you
Moonlight, sunlight, heart-warming glow
Felt with a passion of deep, roaming flow

Exquisition and beauty is all that I see
So deep within you I know it will be
Years have flown by and our light of love shines
Still radiant, magic, blowing our minds

I love you,
Julie,
You're the light of my life

You're wonderful, marvellous
I'm proud you're my wife
So, if I've done wrong in your eyes then I'll see
But believe me my Darling forever we'll be.

Steve Randell

DEAR MUM

You mean the world to me
In everything you do
I think about you all the time
Though I'm far away from you
A simple life is what we know
Material things don't matter
Love is more important to us
As well as a real good natter.

N Carruthers

HERE'S TO MY NEXT FRIEND!

I don't know yet who you will be!
I guess I'll have to wait and see!
You might be rich, you might be poor -
I don't know what God has in store!
You might be strong, you might be weak -
You're what you are and quite unique!
You might be English, born and bred
Or come from somewhere else instead!
You might play draughts, you might play chess,
I hope, at least, you say your prayers!
You might write poems now and then
With silver tongue and golden pen -
Or paint with oils scenes of grace
Then give your pictures pride of place!
Perhaps you sing or act or dance -
With confidence you might advance!
You may have hidden talents now
Till God reveals His will somehow!
The future's there, unwritten yet,
There, till the first day that we've met,
There, till the moment we shake hands . . .
How can we know God's precious plans?
I'm looking forward, patiently,
When I meet you and you meet me!
Look out for me, let's both be kind . . .
I hope this poem comes to mind . . .
The hope within my heart is true!
Here's to my next friend . . . God bless you!

Denis Martindale

DAD

I try to imagine life without you,
The thought is hard to bear,
With your smiling face and gentle voice,
The way you always care,
You're so loving and sharing,
Without you there will be no-one to talk to,
No-one to help us see things through,
Ooh why, Ooh why Dad is it always you
Who is the one that is ill?
You have to see doctors and take tablets,
All of which I wonder is against your will,
After all Dad would you be here today
If it wasn't for us?
How I wish I could say how much you mean to us,
We're trying to be strong for you,
We love you so dear, we know you think of us
And are always near,
So when you feel it's time to go,
Remember we'll be there in your disguise,
The meaning of life we'll all realise,
Then we can too let our feelings show,
But just for now I want you to know how
Much we love you Dad.

Danielle Gallagher

MEMORY LANE

It's Christmastime once again
My heart walks down memory lane,
Thinking of times long ago,
Children playing and rolling in the snow,
Snuggling down on Christmas Eve,
In Father Christmas we did believe
Now as I look at the decorated tree,
There is a touch of sadness for me,
I'd like to pick up the phone,
To see if you were home,
I shed another tear sister dear,
Because I know you're not here,
Instead I look up to the heavens above,
And whisper Happy Christmas my love.

Jaqueline Adams

UNTITLED

Though apart, against our hearts
Perchance that we shall be
In fields of snow this Christmas Eve
Awhile, the morn to greet.

Will you warm me back to life
'Neath Christmas Angels' wings
One bright star our only light
'Til dawn the daytime brings?

A robin will bring mistletoe
Then as your lips touch mine
Hoar frost will melt and white doves soar
In joy, for e'er entwined.

If Christmas Day I wake alone
Look out beyond a dream
A robin will bring mistletoe
Doves cluster in the eves.

I send you love this Christmastime
And know you love me too
Please come and warm me back to life
'Neath eves and mistletoe.

Maggie-Amelia Nixon

ODE TO BARBARA (MY WIFE)

(To my wife Barbara, whom I love dearly)

Thou art more lovelier to me,
Than this visage of mine could be,
I have worshipped thee from near and far,
As the planets bask in shadows of distant stars.
I've watched thee stroll at thy leisure,
Thy voice cascades, like music to my pleasure.

I've seen the pity in thine eyes,
Thy smile, like the sun, lights up the skies.
I've pressed my body close to thine,
Ran my fingers through hair, soft and fine,
My head has rested upon thy breast,
For with thy love, I have been blest.

To bask in the beauty of one so dear,
To be married to that beauty all these years,
All those years and yet no one can say,
I have not loved you, each and every day,
Love is a chain forged of the strongest steel,
My love for you will forever be real.

Nicholas Maughan

To My Husband

My other half is my better half,
He makes my life complete,
Now that's not an easy job,
In fact it's quite a feat.

Twenty years we've been together,
And still I wouldn't part,
I love him very much,
The guy who stole my heart.

His eyes are not just blue,
To me they're sapphire,
I only have to look at them,
To set my soul on fire.

Okay he's not Mr Universe,
That I don't contest,
I like him the way he is,
To me he's the very best.

Some grow tired of their man,
But me I wouldn't swap,
He's not at the bottom of my list,
He's at the very top.

Pauline Uprichard

EMMA
(Dedicated to Emma Russell)

Tonight,
Beneath the stars,
I see the moonlight,
Shining like a pool of silver in your eyes,
Like a mystical star,
Quiet and beautiful,
Tranquil in simplicity,
Placid and soothing
I see your face,
As your lips roll into a smile,
As you show joy,
As you giggle softly,
Quietly,
Like a hiss in the breeze,
Like wind in the trees,
Your priceless voice,
Lovely,
True,
Soft,
Angelic,
Exquisite,
Your golden hair,
Flowing lightly,
Sweet strands of honey in the pale moonlight,
Glowing in radiance
Harmonious,
Brilliant,
Emma, you mean so much to me.

Duncan Roberts

DEDICATED TO

Although we were close, but now so far away
My thoughts will be with you on Christmas day
Thinking of you, even to this festival season
And thinking the way we were, I am about to mention

When the morn was young and the sun smiled through
We walked hand in hand, through the morning dew
Daffodils were in blossom through those sunny hours
Lilac covered the trees, with help from light showers

Whenever I hear the blessings through the air
Listening to the sweet birds sing their praise with care
Reminds me of the summer months, so hot and lazy
When the gold of the sun shone, and days were hazy

When autumn months were still bright and burning
From green, yellow to bronze, the leaves were turning
As winter stepped in, the high winds blew again
White snow settled, as icicles laid on the window pane

You held me close on the Christmas Eve night
Turning the chestnuts over, on he open firelight
Singing Christmas carols together, with good will and cheer
It reminds me of a loved one, as this season draws near

So, whatever your thoughts, or wherever you are
Think back to those mixed seasons then wish on a star
So as we are nearing another Christmas festival
My best wishes to you, my loved ones, and all.

Jean McGovern

CHRISTMAS IS HERE

Christmas is here
and I am sad
My best friend Naoko
lives in Japan
Christmas trimmings
and Christmas tree
friends and family all around.
But I am sad
Naoko is in Japan
we used to have such fun
I wish she was here
Merry Christmas Naoko
All my love.

Lisa Bees (12)

AWAITING YOUR RETURN

A lack of contact for so long
Has persuaded me to write.
For Jason I do miss you
And I'm thinking of you this night.

When you get back, you'll realise,
How much things have changed,
But you still have a place in my heart
And I hope you feel the same.

I've moved on now, have new friends,
But love the old ones still.
In the new lands, in which I move,
I have found no one to fill . . .

The gap you left when you went away,
But do you feel the same?
I want to know if your smile is still there,
And would it be there if I came?

Joanna Haywood

CHRISTMAS CHEER TO ONE AND ALL

Let us gather one and all
On this a special day
To celebrate that Christmas is here
For it's that time of year
When everyone may shed a tear
For those who are so very dear
And wish that they could be with us
On this our special day
So let us not be sad
Let's raise our glasses up on high
And share a glass of Christmas cheer
With everyone who cares to call
Merry Christmas one and all.

Sue Peach

UNCLE PETER

Uncle Peter and Aunt Sylvia
Lived with Grandma in Woking
Every year well almost
We went by train there no joking

First to St Pancras
Then via the Piccadilly and Bakerloo
To catch the train to Woking
That departed from Waterloo

My two sisters Debbie and Jackie
Once drew up komik(e)s about
Peter going 'bub' and Grandma going 'eew bew'
Or else 'bee bar Borneo' where Peter worked about

Then one day in October 1990
Uncle Peter passed away
Into the resurrection
As described in Revelation

Grandma is now in Leominster
Widow Sylvia is still in Woking
Though Peter is gone from cancer
It was not through smoking.

H G Griffiths

IF - AT CHRISTMAS

If mother were here with me sitting underneath this beautiful
Christmas tree
I would be so very happy, laughing merrily as I sip with her some
rose hip tea.
I would tell her how much I love her, thank her for being a
good, caring soul
And hold her hand in mine as we snuggle up inside against
outside's cold.

If mother were here with me and not overseas, many miles away
I would ask her to kneel with me and bow our heads and pray
I would suggest that we thank Mary for bringing Baby Jesus
into this world
And give praise and thanks to the good Lord for giving her the
strength to mother me - her little girl.

If mother were here making jam, Christmas puddings and practising
carols with the choir
I would demand my share of her time and open our gifts as we sit
by the fire
I would let her know that this rounded human being is a result of
her love, care and devotion
Such a shame that I can't tell her this as she is on the other side of
the ocean.

If at Christmas I were able to dine with her, sip champagne
and eat caviar
I would tell her that I thank her for being a superb mother as I follow
that shining star
I would embrace her and let her know that she is greatly treasured
in my heart
And that we should arrange to be together always at Christmas - never
to be separated - never to be again apart.

Margaret Andrews

DEDICATED TO STEVE

Oh Steve you are so appealing
Sweet you are
Our romance is enchanting,
It is captivating by far.
I dedicate this poem to you
You make me feel glad,
If I feel blue.
Instead of feeling sad.
With all my heart it is you I adore.
You are dedicated and true.
I could not wish for more.
I am so fond of you.
Please don't ever leave.
Our love is so strong.
In you I believe.
Don't let it ever go wrong.
You are loyal to me,
Faithful and true.
My darling Steve I'll never leave you.

Jacqueline Darts

Season's Greetings To Syndey My Old Mate

Here's wishing you what you wish me
Season's greetings to you all
I hope your turkey is as dry as old shoe leather
and your stuffing is burnt as well
may your Brussels sprouts be like bullets
and your roast potatoes be like rocks
may the rest of your veggies be like mush
and your Christmas pudding be under-cooked
and your custard be like dog sick
I so on your pathway the other day
may your wine be off and your beer be flat
and I hope your cracker does not crack
and if you get a present it won't be from me
so here's wishing you what you wish me
and I hope your New Year is crappy too
I know you don't have a sore bum or haemorrhoids
because you are a perfect arsehole, unlike me
I don't see why I should have all the fun
so keep on taking the pills just like me
keep your bowels open and put your trust in God
and you won't go far wrong take a tip from me
God bless you my children and may all your troubles be
little ones and I hope they all have good looks like me.

From Donald and them lot who live with me
and she who must be obeyed the wife.

Donald Jay

TO MY DEAR FRIEND

Dear friend I really love you
More than words can say
And that is how it will remain
Until my dying day.

I dream of you almost every night
You snuggle in
I hold you tight
And we're in heaven till morning light.

You're spoken for, I know that's true
So perhaps I'm being unfair.
But I cannot help the way I feel
Deep love is always there.

I've often told you I adore you
And you have given your sweetest smile
I know you can never come to me
Throughout the sands of time.

In my eyes you're drop dead gorgeous
And forever you will be
Till the sun no longer shines
On deep rivers and the sea.

Keith Wilson

To My Guiding Lights

Since the sickness, my teeth have been sharp;
too eager to snap, no candidate for harp,
a snarl has come too quick to my lips,
abrasive words too prone to rip -
yet you stand beside me all the while!

When medication seems to drain sense -
my frustrated tongue tumbling at the first fence;
mind in a hollow, anger nearby,
unsure whether to laugh or cry -
only you calm tantrums with a smile!

Now . . . this Christmas nearly upon us -
a time when sorrow visits like Dickens' ghosts -
mumbling 'Humbug' won't hold tears at bay;
yet all are laid to rest when you say,
'God is with us, walk another mile!'

I do . . . and it is true,
it is he who holds salvation;
to my guides this dedication -
my soul would have died but for you!

Phoenix Martin

HAPPY CHRISTMAS SHANE
(Dedicated to my son Shane)

Happy Christmas my son
You are in my thoughts today
I think about you all the time
Especially on Christmas Day.

It seems such a long time
That we have been apart
But I just wanted to say
I keep you close to my heart.

I send this Christmas message
Especially for you
To tell you how much I love you
And how much I miss you.

Annette Carver